GALLIPOLI,

Cape Helles, April, 1915.

I0200572

The Tragedy of

" The Battle of the Beaches"

Together with the proceedings of H.M.S. "IMPLACABLE."

including the Landings on X. and W. Beaches.

CAPTAIN HUGHES C. LOCKYER, C.B. R.N.

The Naval & Military Press Ltd

❖

Published by
The Naval & Military Press Ltd
Unit 10 Ridgewood Industrial Park,
Uckfield, East Sussex,
TN22 5QE England
Tel: +44 (0) 1825 749494
Fax: +44 (0) 1825 765701
www.naval-military-press.com
www.military-genealogy.com
www.militarymaproom.com

*In reprinting in facsimile from the original, any imperfections are inevitably reproduced
and the quality may fall short of modern type and cartographic standards.*

Revised November 1936

21st ANNIVERSARY.

Dedicated to
The Glorious 29th Division.

Boats Crews and Beach Parties of His Majesty's Navy.

"Theirs not to reason why,
Theirs but to do and die ;
Into the Valley of Death
Rowed the Three Thousand."

With apologies to Lord Tennyson,

- By -

"IMPLACABLE"

INTRODUCTION.

Although many books on the Gallipoli Campaign have been written during the last 21 years, I have found no mention of the fatal mistake made four days before the landings—the cause of the terrible casualties suffered by the 29th Division, neither is it mentioned in the Official histories of the war.

I refer to the sudden alteration of orders issued to the covering squadrons, "to shell the coast ridges," instead of the beaches, as stated in the Naval and Military General orders issued and the Final Battle Orders dated the 17th and 19th April.

I have often been asked to compile a short history of the part played by the "Implacable" during the campaign. In 1933 I received a letter from an officer of High rank at Aldershot who was about to give a lecture on the Gallipoli landings at C. Helles, in which he asked me "Did Implacable shell X beach without orders" to which I replied "Yes" and. "No" as I had told Admiral Wemyss on the 21st April that it was my intention to shell X beach as the boats went in."

This officer was observation officer on board of H.M.S. Albion at V beach.

Again in 1935 I was asked by a writer of Naval Histories if I would supply him with material for a book on Gallipoli he was

about to write " before the present generation has passed away."
I supplied him with everything I could, as a small contribution
towards the mass of information supplied by officers and others,
to help him in his compilation of historical facts worthy of being
handed down to future generations such as maps, photographs,
yarns, comic and otherwise, together with a full detailed history **specially asked for** ; it is a most charming book, he published everything I sent him except the full "detailed history"
which contained the tragedy of " Swapping Horses ! ! "

Now, having read " Gallipoli, the fading vision " by John
North, 1936, I can see no reason why the true history of the
" Battle of the Beaches " should not be completed and published, if only to prevent the future students of Military History
at the Staff College, Camberley, from jumping up and exclaiming
in strong language " My God, Why the — didn't they shell the
beaches ! "

I have included in these memoirs

1.   Extracts from the journal of Mr. H. R. Tate, Midshipman,
H.M.S. Implacable, 1915.

2.   A letter of appreciation from General Sir Ian Hamilton
to the Ships Company of H.M.S. Implacable.

3.   A letter published in the Cambridge Weekly News 1915
from Stoker Petty Officer C. R. Cook of the same ship.

A most interesting letter describing the events from when
the troops came on board on the 24th April, until they were
landed the next morning.

He was an eye witness of the happenings on W. Beach;
**curiously enough he makes the same remarks as those of Captain
Clayton of the Lancashire Fusiliers,** which seems to point to the
fact, that the troops who had been practicing the landings at
Port Moudros, Lemnos Id., and had probably been told that the
beaches would all be shelled before the boats went in— never

knew that the orders had been altered. Consequently they went straight into a death trap—and in spite of everything—conquered—Heroes All.

Years afterwards, a celebrated First Lord of the Admiralty during the war, talking things over with one of my officers, remarked " Had all ships done the same, history might have been very different." Mr. John North's book seems to agree.

An appreciation.—On the moblization of the " Second Fleet " for war. The Cadets of the Royal Naval College Dartmouth, were distributed among these ships, most of which were sent to Gallipoli, being as " somebody " remarked of little monetary value, my ship I believe was valued at £40,000. Shortly after war was declared, the Cadets were all rated midshipmen ; these were either in charge of boats at the landings, or belonged to the various " Beach parties." There is only one word for them all, they were " Splendid " and their ages ranged between 16½ to 17½ years ! !

Personally, I simply carried out what I had learnt at the Staff College, Camberley, in 1913—the success of the actual operations being entirely due to my gunnery officer, the late Commander J. W. Scott, D.S.O.

HUGHES C. LOCKYER.

The Hill,   CAPTAIN H.M.S. IMPLACABLE, 1915.
   Langport,
     Somerset,   April 25th., 1936.

OFF CAPE HELLES.

MARCH 28th TO APRIL 24th 1915.

During this period the ship was employed in observation duties off C. Helles—opening fire on any likely positions, enemy batteries and trenches. Points selected were coast ridges in the valleys, solitary buildings, etc. The ship laying off during the night. On one occasion we went in at night and shelled Seddul Bahr by order of Admiral — steaming in slowly until abreast the town. All search lights were switched on and the beach (V) and vicinity examined—not a man to be seen. We then shelled the place, search lights being used from the Asiatic side They were shelled also, and immediately turned off (see page 13).

We were occupied on this job for nine or ten days taking turns with other ships—and only saw three men during the whole period. They were running poles—probably field telephones across the road, south of Achi Baba and disappeared in the direction of a position we had already shelled a day or two before.

1. Shortly after the Implacable returned to Port Moudros, a meeting was called on board H.M.S. Euryalus—Admiral Wemyss. The captains of the ships detailed for landing the troops attended—on the 21st April, at this time the orders of :—

    (1)   General Sir Ian Hamilton's original orders.

    (2)   G.O.C. 29th Division, dated 19th April.

    (3)   Admiral Wemyss' Memorandum dated 17th April

All stated that " **all the beaches** " would be bombarded before the landing took place.

After the Admiral had gone over all the details of the orders he asked if any captain had any proposition to make before closing the meeting. I then said " As Implacable is the only one remaining under weigh during the landing, I propose disposing my tows on either beam, accompanying the tows as far as possible and she.ling the beach on the way in. To which the Chief of Staff, a gunnery expert remarked in a very decisive manner " You will never be able to pick up the range quick enough "— I, not being an expert remained silent. The Admiral then said " You have all heard what has been stated I leave the matter entirely in the hands of my Captains and I know you will all do your best for the success of the operations."

On the same day **the order for the other ships to anchor was cancelled**—but I am afraid the chief of staffs remark carried a great influence.

2.   On returning to my ship my gunnery officer came to me and reported that he had been sent for to attend another meeting held on board I think, H.M.S. Swiftsure which was attended by Royal Artillery Officers—and at which it was decided that instead of shelling the beaches the bombarding ships would shell the coast ridge. and other selected points. He had been sent for because of the observation work we had carried out. He gave them all the information he could, and remarked that he did not always understand the reasons I had for shelling particular places, in fact told them practically that **you could make out nothing to shoot at,** and his opinion, as stated to me was that the bombardment would be practically valueless, which it proved to be, especially, as in the interval between bombardment and landings three-quarters to one hour gave the enemy time to recover from the shock.

3. The orders that the beaches were to be bombarded in Admiral Wemyss' " Memorandum " **were never cancelled,** consequently the captains of the attendant ships probably saw no necessity to take advantage of the order that they could remain under weigh and shell the beaches themselves if they wished to.

There being only three days before sailing and all the Infantry G.O.C.'s being afloat this sudden alteration of orders probably never reached them in time to protest—as I imagine they all would have done. Neither did I ever hear of it officially. I don't suppose a case of " Swapping Horses " has ever occurred before that led to such disastrous results.—**I happen to know that the General Commanding-in-Chief is in full agreement with me here.**

4. It was reported in the official Dispatches that X Beach was much more adaptable for shelling than the other beaches. I can quite understand this statement being made at the time as a matter of policy—as by the time they arrived the enormous losses incurred and the situation at Gallipoli made it necessary. This statement is most inaccurate as the other beaches had a gentle slope up to the coast ridges to a distance of 300 to 400 yards. At X beach from the water to the steep cliff was only 25 yards. Ships could have approached the other beaches and shelled the whole of the area from the water line to the back slope with the greatest of ease by two ships going in with a fixed sight, guns fan shape across the bow, which has the advantage of being able to set all the fuzes beforehand—or by various other methods.

By the report of Captain Clayton Lancs. Fusiliers, he was evidently still under the impression that the W Beach had been bombarded but the shots went too high. Referring to the bombardment he states " **We thought nothing could live but as a**

matter of fact they bombarded too far inland, the trenches over-looking the landing beaches were not touched."

5. Anything I did successfully in these operations I can only put down to the fact that in 1913 the Senior Officers Course at the War College Portsmouth attended a fortnights Course at the Staff College, Camberley, on amphibious warfare where it was impressed upon us that no landing should be attempted until the covering ships had thoroughly shelled the beaches and their approaches and they rapped it in on every occasion possible. So much did the G.O.C. 29th Division rely on the Bombardment of the beaches that, in the Memo of 19th April, it states that **this would be done twice,** firstly at daybreak and secondly as the boats proceeded to the beaches in line abreast.

Consequently it is hard to believe that the original idea of altering these tactics emanated from the Military Staff.

In the Official History Military Operations 1929, page 218—The bombardment of the beaches is still stated as having taken place. Extraordinary as it may seem everything seems to point to the fact that the change in tactics never reached " General Head Quarters " on board of S.S. Arcadian then laying at Port Moudros also.

THE NIGHT ATTACK ON SEDDUL BAHR.

From the journal of Mr. H. R. Tate, Midshipman, 7th April, 1915 :—
"At 21.00 we again entered the Dardanelles steering by the buoy (a small light buoy had been dropped during the day) and trained the port guns on Seddul Bahr, engines were stopped, and absolute silence maintained. Then the fun started. All searchlights suddenly switched on, those on the far side waving in the air so as to dazzle the enemy. Every gun that would bear blazed out to port, the bark of the 12 prs. and the crash of

the 6 inch made an unholy din. In the village the shells were bursting, great dull red flashes, with the glimpse of houses falling like a pack of cards. Men and horses were seen running frantic- ally round and their yells could be heard plainly. Suddenly a Turk switched on from the Asiatic side but a salvo from the starboard guns put it out, meanwhile Seddul Bahr was well on fire, so "cease fire" was sounded and we retired gracefully. Turkish Cavalry apparently chose Seddul Bahr to rest in at night This ought to learn 'em !!

200 shells were fired by port guns and four shells from star- board."

" THE LANDING."
April 25th, 26th, 27th to May 20th, 1915.

The main force started from Moudros, at 4 p.m. 24th Apri' arriving off Cape Helles at daylight.

State of sea, calm; weather, calm b.c.

Having taken up position on the correct bearing of X Beach distance three miles, the troops were then embarked in the transport boats and formed up in tow of four picket boats, two on each side—abreast of after funnel, another two tows formed up on starboard side, these containing troops for W Beach.

Whilst the boats were taking station, the starboard anchor was eased down and cable veered to 1½ shackles, the cable was then stoppered to the riding bitts with three inch lashings and half a shackle ranged ready for running—so that. The stopper carried away on the anchor taking the ground. This was done owing to the probable inaccuracy of the chart, and the certainty of getting in as close as possible without risk—the engines being put to full speed astern directly the stopper parted.   (See note 1).

The necessary instructions having been given to the gun-layers about their individual targets and method of attack, all gunsights were set to 1,800 yards. The starboard upper deck six inch casemate gun was also to be used for indicating the fall of shot as the ship approached the land. The six inch guns were ordered to fire five rounds rapid, fore turret five rounds from each gun as quickly as loaded quick firing 12 pr. rs to open fire when heavy gun firing ceased.

At 5.30 a.m. the ship proceeded in at 5 knots, at 2,500 yards reduced to slow and started ranging with the six inch casemate U.D. Gun with fixed sight 1,800—the fall of shot gradually approaching the beach. The 8th shot struck water about 200 yards from beach and " open fire " sounded and engines were stopped.—The first rounds of six in. guns burst over the water about 10 yards from the beach. After the rapid fire was over the sights were then raised as necessary and when the firing ceased the boats proceeded in, followed by the ship using the Q.F. guns long the ridges until the boats were disembarking the troops. The ship brought up with 6½ fathoms under her stem about 500 to 600 yards from the shore. (See Plan).

When within about 1,000 yards from shore heavy rifle fire was directed at the fore bridge and fore lower top.

I did not notice it at first as we were inside the sandbag redoubt erected on " Monkey Island " i.e., Standard Compass platform to protect that instrument from shrapnel fire. However suddenly the gunnery officer Lieut. Com. Scott seized his nose as if a wasp had stung him and said " My God, what's that?" I am afraid I laughed and shouted " Down Heads!" suddenly realizing that the wasps were made of lead.

The redoubt consisted of a breastwork two feet thick covered by a roof with oak beams, across which were laid all the spare brass condenser tubes lent by the Engineer commander (on conditions that he could have any if required ! !) over this were sandbags—to which is attached a story.

On my way down Channel I was ordered to Spithead for 24 hrs. and signalled ahead requesting Dockyard Staff to come out and cut off the ends of my bridges—also requesting two truck loads of sand and 800 sandbags. The reply came back from C-in-C—bridge work approved—sand etc. not approved—with a sort of witty remark such as " Why take coals to New-castle." I replied back requesting permission to pay for sand etc. demanded as I am " the person who is going to be shot at " (of course I knew C-in-C). I got my stuff and a lucky thing too as things turned out.

Ammunition expended during this operation—
   12 inch guns   10 rounds common shell.
    6 inch guns   179 rounds Common and Lyddite.
   12 pounders   154 rounds Common and Lyddite.

Having seen that the disembarkation was going on most satisfactorily, the ship then proceeded to its appointed anchorage off Cape Tekeh between X and W beaches and shortly after-wards we had the pleasure of seeing the Fusiliers attack " Hill 114 " at the back of the Cape with great success, the enemy surrendering in considerable numbers. (See note 3).

Steps were now taken to get the ranges of various points visible from the ship—one especially being a solitary mushroom headed tree on the ridge at the back of the coast ridge, which ran North and South and named " Lone Tree Hill." During the afternoon the enemy made a heavy attack on Hill 114. They advanced in lines straight across Lone Tree Hill—as they passed the tree, were received with rapid fire (lyddite and com-mon) from the six in. guns which stopped the advance. At the same time a field battery opened fire on the R. Fusiliers holding lines in front of X Beach on which fire was opened. Although we could not see our shell bursting in the valley it was put out of action and we saw the horses with unoccupied limbers galloping back towards Krithia. The afternoon attack then dwindled down. (See note 4).

By a piece of luck our anchorage was in the inshore counter current running down the coast which kept our head North and the Ship broadside on to the shore so saving any necessity for using springs on the cable.

At midnight the enemy again made a fierce attack on Hill 114 (Teke-Burnu) and we received a signal from X Beach that they were " very hard pressed." The only point of aim we had was where the star shell rose and fell behind the coast ridge and the range of the " Mushroom Tree" which was behind the enemy, We opened fire at the coast ridge sky line and worked the guns along this area setting the sights for the shell to drop in the valley.—We fired 60 rounds of six in Common Shell and the attack ceased gradually. By this time Lt. Comdr. Scott and myself were feeling it a bit as our shell were bursting out of sight of the ship and we got no signals. However we did not have much time to think about it, for a short time after we ceased firing, a signal from General Marshall was received, " We are heavily engaged, can you give us support " at about 1.30 a.m. (See note 5)

This was a different proposition as instead of firing over the heads of our troops from behind, in this case our fire was parallel to the line we calculated the troops had occupied, extending from W to V beaches. We were greatly helped by the star shells, as their line of ascent was at right angles to our gun fire. We opened fire in the same manner as before aiming at the point where the star shells disappeared behind the ridge; the sights were adjusted as necessary to extend along the line and back again distributing the shell by altering the training of the guns slightly to the left the idea being to cover an elongated oval extending from the back of W beach to behind V. As I received no complaints or further signals, we ceased firing at 3.35 a.m. when the firing ashore practically ceased. We expended 150 rounds of six inch Common Shell during this attack. As *General Marshall was wounded I heard nothing more about this interesting episode, but some time afterwards I was told that the Implacable's guns on that night saved the situation, and I wish to put on record that owing to the seamen ratings being away on Transport duties, all the six inch guns were manned by Marines and Stokers under Captain L. Norcock, R.M.L.I. who was in command of the battery and whose valuable services were brought to the notice of the C-in-C Admiral De Robeck.

During the forenoon of the 26th all boats were sent to Y beach for re-embarking the troops the position having been ordered to be evacuated. It was reported to me that this was done without a shot being fired, the Marines who had dug themselves in on the high coast ridge still occupying their trenches until they discovered that the evacuation of the other troops was in progress. There was not an enemy in sight—a terrible mess up. (See note 6).

After this date ship's gunfire was directed by orders from shore stations ; with the exception of occasional night firing which I did on my own responsibility, having observed that the enemy during daytime never walked on the main road which crossed the sky line on the Southern slope of Achi Baba but invariably crossed it under cover of the scrub on either side in small groups. The Krithia—Cape Helles road just south of the village—was also shelled, the routine being to change the hour of opening fire each time. Later on fire was also opened on the ridges between Y beach and Krithia. (See note 7).

*Reported.

THE DEFENCES OF X BEACH.

According to the official records the beach had a guard of 12 men which was all that was necessary, as other troops were in the vicinity. On being occupied it was found that it was also defended by two four barrelled one inch, Nordenfelts on timber mountings which commanded the wide stretch of the beach but which had been disabled by gun fire.—These were "at the ready" with hoppers in position and spare hoppers (filled) by each gun. The firing levers were bent, otherwise the guns were in good order.

Although there was no barbed wire defence the Beach itself was protected by a line of reefs invisible from seaward which extended practically its whole length and about 25 yards from the shore, the boats grounded on this, the troops then having to wade ashore, consequently as these guns fired four half-pound steel projectiles at a time and 30 aimed rounds a minute, there would have been very little chance of the boats getting in before being waterlogged in deep water ; incidentally as one projectile would easily have killed six men, in line at a time, the casualties would have been enormous, and the success of the operation very doubtful if they had not been disabled. (See Plan II.)

One of these guns is now at Hounslow Barracks the depot of the Royal Fusiliers, the other at the Royal Naval Barracks, Plymouth.

THE LANDINGS AT X AND W BEACHES.

From the journal of Mr. H. R. Tate, Midshipman, 25th April, 1915·

"At about 3.45 a.m. the ship stopped and the boats came alongside and were given fannies of hot cocoa, and filled up with troops. All very cold and expectant, at about 4 a.m. we heard heavy firing and saw flashes away to the North, then the whole fleet suddenly blazed out, a wonderful sight, and this continued till daylight when we began to close the beach and things got warmer ; there was a whine overhead and a large shell fell far astern by the "Dartmouth". Then one came down about five yards away and drenched us and caused a good deal of bad language. All this time we were approaching the beach, the ship with her anchor hanging down. When she reached 500 yards she went astern and anchored and we went out of her shelter into the open ; the blast of the 12 inch over our heads was most unpleasant, as were the bullets which were now coming down all round like little wasps.

The next beach (W) appeared to be mined well and the boats were having a rotten time. The whole peninsular was a mass of bursting shell and flame.

According to plan the picket boat slipped us and we landed our little load. I was on the extreme left and found a sandy patch and got right in, third boat ashore, nearly all the rest ran on a reef about 20 yards out and the troops had to jump overboard and swim. As we touched land one of our 12 inch shell hit the cliff just overhead and filled the boat with earth. I thought we had been mined personally. (Note—This is probably correct as the ship was then only firing Q.F. 12 prs.—H. C. L.)

We then pulled out to trawlers, which had got in closer than the ship could, and embarked more troops, on my third trip, went aground on the point and we formed rather a tempting target for some Turks in a trench whom we could see firing quite plainly ; we were hit several times but none hurt. I eased off my revolver in their direction but didn't do much damage beyond nearly falling overboard. Finally we floated again, we landed boatload after boatload till about 10 a.m. and then hauled off to the ship for a rest. No one killed in my boat. After about half an hour we started to land men on W. Beach. Here the casualties had been bad, and over a hundred dead were on the beach alone, while the sand was all stained with blood, a derelict cutter full of dead, and water-logged, formed a basis for a temporary pier. About 50 Turks suddenly appeared overhead, fired at us and then surrendered. Four of our men found a sniper in the cliff and bayonetted him and chucked him over the cliff, all his insides came out. A subaltern and three men tried to locate some other snipers who were firing at us, but each in turn gave little starts and fell down dead. One was wounded and staggered towards us crying, a man wounded in the leg saw a pal hit nearby, so hopped over and picked him up and came towards the beach with his leg trailing behind. Then he was killed.

Several of our men are wounded, a bullet found a billet in the stomach of our surgeon Forrester and killed him. We were in a group on the quarter deck when he was shot and he just collapsed quite quietly.

We have landed about 16,000 (?) men and have had 400 killed down our end. It would appear that the place is not impregnable after all ! ! Towards evening I got towed with two other boats to S.S. Andania (B6) where I went inboard and joined a Lieutenant Green from Q.E. whose job was to unload stores and land them. I looked out for the eight men from Implacable and took over big lighters and horse boats.

The Turks made a terrific counter attack and broke through to the very cliff tops, but the beach parties joined in and drove them back. The Royal Fusiliers advanced too far and got enfiladed."

ENVOI.

The alteration of the orders to shell the beaches resulted in delaying the advance for four days at least, by that time the 29th. Division had received nearly 4,000 casualties, and the loss of officers was enormous ; for example the 2nd. Battalion Royal Fusiliers, the regiment we landed without a casualty, had the Colonel wounded, eleven officers either killed or wounded and the regiment had between 300 or 400 other casualties in killed or wounded.

This delay allowed the enemy to bring up their forces and the first battle of Krithia fought at the end of the month, was a failure.

This probably altered the course of the whole Campaign.

FINIS.

NOTES.

1. No spar was used as stated in Official History, this being an impossible operation. Col. Newenham mistook our "mine rake" bowsprit as having something to do with it—also see his report of landing and page 91 in "With the 29th Division" by Creighton.

2. Firing orders wrongly stated by Ashmead Bartlett. He was not there and got hold of the wrong yarn. See his "Uncensored Dardanelles" and in other publications Wemyss etc.

3. Shortly after anchoring Fleet Surgeon Forrestor was killed on the quarter deck just as he was leaving to take charge of a beach station for evacuating the wounded to the Hospital ships—he had just shifted into khaki and was talking to three of us in blue "Kismit" Other casualties in boats during the day, 1 killed, 5 wounded.

4. See Campaign in "Gallipoli" Hans Kannengcesser Pasha G.O.C. Krithia (25th April 1915).

5. These night operations not mentioned in official history of the war—see page 31 "With the 29th Division." At the time we opened fire over X Beach the Royal Fusiliers had been driven in almost to the cliffs at the back of X beach and had suffered heavily, most of their officers being either killed or wounded. Their Colonel Newenham was wounded badly in the afternoon but carried on after first aid dressing. Our shell must have been passing over just clear of their heads.

6. During the afternoon of the 25th from our fore bridge we could see a regular string of troops from Y beach landing, wandering up towards Krithia and getting pretty close to it. Shortly afterwards they began straggling back apparently in

no formation whatever. I think the Turks must have laid "dogo" for during their return they touched them up with rifle fire and our men picked up the double. However they had wasted a lot of time—the enemy's forces gradually increasing (The Turkish G.O.C. a German General was in Krithia at the time and concentrated all troops available to attack). The only intimation that we had that the troops at Y beach were trying to connect up with X was the arrival of a bugler boy of the Scottish Borderers who wandered in to X beach and on being questioned replied that he was looking for curios. I don't know if he was a wag, but he had evidently lost himself. The regiment during the evening was decimated by the enemy so he was lucky.

7. "Birnam Woods begin to move." On the attack on Achi Baba on May 5th our signalman reported "that the sky line between Gully Beach and Krithia was moving about." This turned out to be a line of men togged up in bushes. They were greeted with a few rounds of six inch shell—apparently snipers taking station. There is a photo of one in Keyes Memoirs.

IMPLACABLE "DESERTERS."

After the landing beaches had more or less settled down, it was found that we had four men missing from the beach parties —this was passed along. A few days afterwards a boat came alongside and deposited the four men dressed in mixed uniform of Royal Fusiliers and Lancashire Fusiliers. On being brought before me they all had broad grins. On being asked why they had left the beach, the reply was :— "We couldn't help it, Sir—we had to— " but said one, "We had a hell of a time—." They had been in the front line for a week ! ! So all I could do was to congratulate them on being alive.

LETTER FROM SIR IAN HAMILTON.

Letter of thanks to the Ships Company of H.M.S. "Implacable" for gifts of Tobacco etc. Collected and despatched in five cases by H. PAYMAN, A.B., and D. HUDSON, A.B. Dictated.

> General Headquarters,
> Mediterranean Expeditionary Force,
> Gallipoli.
> 21st September, 1915.

DEAR SIR,

I have to-day sent you a cable acknowledging the splendid gift the ships company of H.M.S. " Implacable " have sent to our troops now fighting on the Gallipoli Peninsular. I have also taken all measures to let the generous gift be known throughout our forces, and all of us here are, I assure you, much touched at this most pleasing evidence you have given us of your friendship and sympathy. You of the "Implacable " who have shared with us our dangers and adventures realise the tough job we are up against in the Dardanelles, in a way impossible to the ordinary people at home. All goes well, but it is a slow business and certainly it would do us good to hear once more the thunder of the big guns of the "Implacable."—A ship whose motto in conflict with the enemy was always :—

" NEARER THE BETTER.

With my best salaams to all your Gallant Ships Company.

> Believe me, Yours truly,
>
> (Signed) IAN HAMILTON.
> (General).

FROM CAMBRIDGE WEEKLY NEWS, JUNE 4th, 1915.

SIR,

I have permission from the censor to send you copies of Force Order and personal note issued by General Ian Hamilton and Major-General Aylmer Hunter-Weston, to the Army before they made their glorious landing on the morning of the 25th : also a few brief notes of what has happened since. The part played by the Implacable in that landing was great, and drew personal praise from Admiral R. E. Wemyss and the Colonel and officers of the Royal Fusiliers, copies of which I have the honour of enclosing.

On the 23rd the troopships began to get a move on, and the send off we gave the Australians and Fusiliers was worth coming out here to hear. The most comical part of the business was when we got under weigh, and passed a Russian cruisers our band played a Scotch tune, and broke into an Irish air as we passed a French Battleship. On the evening of the 24th we received a regiment of Royal Fusiliers and Naval Brigade, whom we were to land in open boats, under cover of our guns, at dawn on the morrow and what fine fellows they were : well seasoned, in the pink of condition, for most of them had already seen service in India, Egypt and Flanders. I had 24 in my mess and you can guess there wasn't much sleep for anyone.

It was interesting to walk round the ship, some asleep, any and everywhere ; others writing Home (the last for a good many poor fellows) and others spinning dits. Everybody was about by 3 a.m. Sunday, 25th, and fell in by 3.45 and how real to see them charge magazines before they embarked. By 4.45 all the fleet had come into line, opposite their respective positions and the bombardment began. We ran close into our beach, and poured salvo after salvo. 12 in. shrapnel searched the cliffs, while 6 in. did ditto to the beach, and you can understand what an 850 lb. shell will do at 1,000 yards range.

Under cover of our fire, our boats made for the beach, and I am happy to say did not lose a single man in landing but naturally suffered heavily in storming and clearing the cliffs. No pen can describe or artist can paint the scene, it was Hades with the lid off on that peninsula. The landing of the troops on the next beach to ours was also splendidly carried out under very heavy fire from the Turks and Co. and a perfect hail of bullets greeted the boats as they came within range (**one wonders how anything could survive the shell fire from the fleet**) I saw hundreds of shots splashing like rain round the boats and it was glorious to see the boys leap out and wade ashore. I will take off my cap to every soldier I pass, for everyone deserves a medal as big as my fat head.

It was something to watch our boys get a footing and dig themselves in. One particular charge was most brilliant. Two shells pitched among a group of Turks and over the ridge came our boys, and we could see the Turks being driven pell-mell down the slope, and we cheered for all we were worth and they answered us back as they went with the bayonet. What was left of the Turks soon held their hands above their heads, and were made prisoners.

Every inch of ground gained since that never-to-be-forgotten Sunday morning has been contested bravely, and finally won by magnificent work and one wonders how we managed it at all.

Up to date the dear old ship has come through splendid. Am sorry to say our Fleet Surgeon has been killed. We bitterly mourn his loss, and the Navy loses one of its brightest officers and one of the finest gentlemen that ever stood in a pair of boots.

Yours etc.,

CHAS. R. COOK.

Stoker Petty Officer

H.M.S. Implacable, Dardanelles.
May, 1915.

[Copyright].

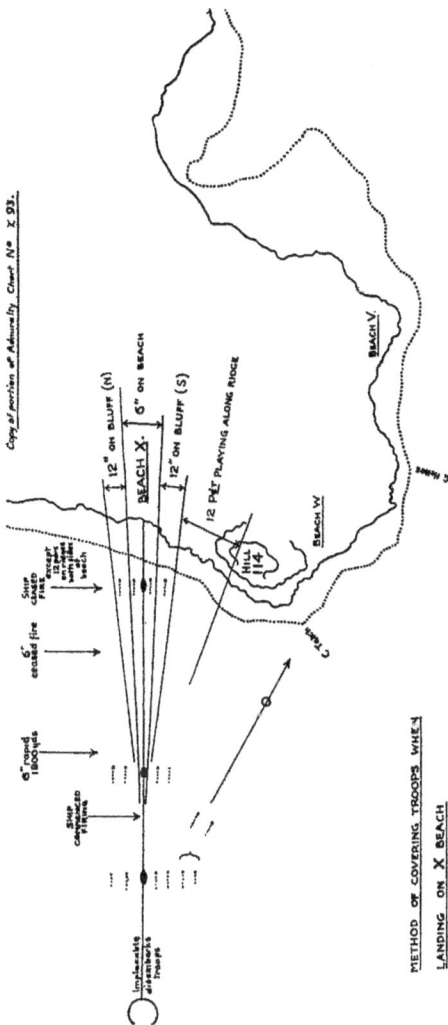

" The Battle of the Beaches."

Copy of portion of Admiralty Chart No X 93.

12" ON BLUFF (N)

6" ON BEACH

BEACH X.

12" ON BLUFF (S)

12 Pdr PLAYING ALONG RIDGE

BEACH V.

BEACH W.

HILL 114

C Helles

C Tekke

Intercept 12 pdrs on right when off beach

Some covered fire

6" cocked fire

6" round 1800 yds

Ship cannonaded shrapnel

Implacable disembark troops

METHOD OF COVERING TROOPS WHEN
LANDING ON X BEACH

H.M.S "Implacable"
25th April, 1915

Scale of yards

Rough Scale 1 inch = 25 yards
Working Plan
of
Implacable Beach.

Soundings in Feet at L.W.O.S.
Variation --- Little or None.
⋯⋯ denotes Sand.
〰 denotes Cliff.
〰〰 denotes Reef or Shoal
Length of possible landing place 40 yards.

Note Steam Pinnaces & Cutters may make the pier or the beach to the Northward at all states of the tide. No landing is possible, South of the pier.

By Lieut Pollhill R.N.
Soundings By
Sub. Lieut Back. R.N.

Approximately

Buoy

Bottom line no Beach

Reef

Shoal Water

Water Boat

Two 1 inch 4 barrelled Q.F guns

Wooden Pier

Motor Boat about here

25 yds

220 yds

Reef

Shoal Water

Reef

Shoal Water

Reef

Pier

Heather and Scrub

Heather and Scrub

Road up Cliff Vo

To N. Beach

+75'

+75'

+75'